WHAT IS YOUR PURPOSE?

DR. CRYSTAL PUGH

ISBN: 978-1-965082-04-1

Publishing By: The Acklin Group

Editing By: DemiCo National, LLC

www.DemiCoNational.com

Table of Contents

Dear Reader,

Discovering your purpose in the midst of your most difficult situations and realizing that God has ordained greater for your life. He wants you to live in His abundant blessings.

I pray that the God of peace and understanding will ignite you into your destiny and purpose and allow you to fulfill your God given purpose.

I pray that the King of Glory will enlighten your eyes to understand and give you revelation of the finished work of Christ Jesus.

I pray that your past has been put behind you and that you will unlock the doors to the greatest manifestations of your future.

I pray that God will place the right people in your path that will help thrust you into your purpose. I pray that your needs will be met as you read through the pages of this book.

I pray that from this day forth fear will no longer control your life and that you walk in the wholeness of your time.

I pray that your purpose in God will manifest blessings and that your life will never be the same but will be greater and fulfilled. In Jesus' name, Amen.

Dr. Crystal

Chapter One

What is Your Kingdom Assignment & Purpose?

If you are reading this book, you may be like the other millions of people on this earth seeking to find their purpose in this world. Not knowing your purpose can breed all types of identity crises and traumas that will in turn invite a host of abusers into your life and into the lives of the people around you. We must first understand that our purpose is not about us and our surroundings, but it is about God using us for His purpose in and throughout our lives.

Before you can excel in growth and be all God wants you to be, you must first know who you are and who God created you to be. Lamentations 3:40 says, "Let us test and examine our ways, and return to the Lord!"

He invites you to get quiet and take time to seek God, and to know thyself.

We were all created for a purpose and we must fulfill this purpose by first being honest with ourselves and then going to God the creator to ask, "What is my purpose?" When we define purpose, it declares the reason for which something is created or for which something exists.

For this very reason we exist today because of His purpose. In Genesis 1:26 God said "Let us make man in our own image." Therefore, we must know and seek to find our purpose here on earth. Seeking the creator is as simple as going to your car dealership to inquire about a problem you are having with your car. They will be able to give you the precise diagnosis because it is all downloaded in the brain of the computer. Before you know it, your car is functioning properly and you are on your way. Why? It is because you went straight to the source.

You must seek the creator to receive proper instruction regarding figuring out and fulfilling the purpose that He has placed within you. However, some people will go to a source that cannot give them true revelation of their purpose because they had nothing to do with its creation. Would you go to your local water company to ask them about an electrical problem you are having in your garage? No, you wouldn't. You would go directly to the source,

Your purpose is an unraveling of a perfect epic idea born in the soul of God. You're on earth for an assignment by God and for God. Your purpose in life is far more awe-inspiring than your personal achievements and accolades.

Your accomplishments in life are pointless if you're not operating on purpose. You're here to do his will and exercise his mandate. God gave you gifts, talents and passions to complement your purpose but your gifts are not your purpose.

Paul wrote in the scriptures, "For we are God's masterpiece. He has created us anew in Christ Jesus, so we can do the good things he planned for us long ago." (Ephesians 2:10 NLT)

You were formed by God to relieve the world of some pain. God completely planned your life out even before your parents were born to provide answers to some problems and add value to the world and in doing so you'll find fulfillment and success.

God Has A Mandated Purpose For You

It is impossible to find purpose outside of God. Everything is centered on God who created the whole world and the millions of species living within it. One of the greatest tests of purpose is daily fulfillment and joy.

The search for the purpose of life has puzzled people for thousands of years. Many have invented their own sense of purpose. Purpose begins with God. We didn't form ourselves, so we're not authorized to create a path for our lives without consulting with our Maker. Allow God to show you the path He has already carved out for you. Like a master woodcarver, He has the chisel in His hand and wisely creates the impressions from His mind in wood for the world to see and emulate.

The bible says, "I will praise You, for I am fearfully and wonderfully made; Marvelous are Your works, and that my soul knows very well." (Psalms 139:14)

He is the perfection of beauty. If you want to have a life of Significance, ask God to reveal to you His purpose for your life.

The concept of purpose is so transformational. Your purpose determines your friendships and those who you allow into your life.

Becoming One With Your Purpose

Your purpose started in God in heaven, and you were sent on an assignment to the earth. Before you think of any plan for your life, know that God had the plans first. He's been waiting for you to awaken to His plans and purpose for your life. You're on a divine assignment to the earth.

If you don't embrace your purpose and uniqueness, you can spend your entire life striving to conform and comparing ourselves to others. By celebrating what makes you different rather than wasting time trying to be like others, you will discover your unique and special gifts. This discovery will lead you to Living Your Truth.

We were all sculpted to be different and unique in our own ways, that's one of the beauties of human existence. Take the time to understand your purpose and then you will be on your way to your divine destiny!

Chapter Two

Pursuing Your Purpose God's Way

There is a scripture in the bible that says, "It is the Glory of God to conceal a matter. But, the glory of kings is to search it out."

Proverbs 25:2. "This refers to the revelation of God's will and purpose for your life, but you must seek it."

For many years I did not know my purpose. I knew that I existed, I knew that there was a God, and I always knew that there was a burning on the inside of me to want more than what my surroundings offered me. I will now share a real-life experience with you. It was the year 1995 and I was in my early twenties.

I had gotten acquainted with this very nice guy and began to fall head over heels in love with him. I honestly believed that this man was going to be my husband and was convinced that we were going to be together the rest of our lives. My fairytale image of the idea of he and I was axed one gloomy day when I found out that he had cheated on me with another young lady.

This young lady had a very cute and distinct short hairstyle. I was devastated and worried myself almost to death, riddled with questions. "Why did he cheat on me?" "What was it about me that made him cheat on me?"

Your Identity In Christ Jesus

Not knowing my purpose birthed an identity crisis. After all the lies and arguments, and beating myself up, I went to the beauty salon and had the beautician cut off all of my beautiful long hair. She begged and pleaded with me not to cut it, but I was persistent in my decision. Once she complied, I had her cut my hair into the same cute, cropped hairstyle that the young lady had, whom my lover had cheated on me with.

The bible says, "I will praise thee; for I am fearfully and wonderfully made marvelous are thy works; and that my soul knoweth right well." (Psalm 139:14)

You are not supposed to try to find purpose on your own. God already has your purpose waiting for you to discover it. Your purpose is found in your assignment. Your assignment is the work that you're to do on the earth. There's a work that you're to do on the earth. You owe a service to humanity by virtue of your purpose and assignment.

In the weakness of my mind and the lowness of the predicament that I was in, I thought that if I cut my hair like hers, it would stop him from cheating. Well, after cutting my hair, dealing with the physical, mental, and emotional trauma from being cheated on by someone that I desperately loved as well as dealing with the disappointment from my mother, for cutting my hair, we still broke up.

Knowing your purpose helps you to be confident in your identity. It is a dangerous thing to live life without knowing who you are.

The bible says, "I can do all things through Christ which strengtheneth me." (Philippians 4:13)

We Must Become One With Our Identity

Over the years I have seen many people, especially broken women, struggle to get their identity back. They try to do it by growing their hair longer, getting new make-up kits, dress better or use the latest perfume to help them feel better about themselves. I was one of them until I found myself in Christ. Your divine purpose and spiritual identity work together to shape you into whom you were born to be in Christ. I used to be unsure of my purpose until I began to understand my true identity in Christ. If you don't know who you are in Christ, you can never understand or discover your purpose.

The bible says, "To whom God would make known what is the riches of the glory of this mystery among the Gentiles; which is Christ in you, the hope of glory:" (Colossians 1:27)

Our Greatest Treasure on Earth is Our Identity in Christ. Our single most valuable –yet least understood– treasure here on earth is our identity in Christ. Until it becomes prominent in our thinking, we remain stuck in the impossible struggle to make our flesh behave. And since it won't behave, others see us as hypocrites trying to act out the role of the Christians –failing to do what we say.

I cannot urge you enough to learn verses about your identity in Christ. Understanding who "you have become" will make a monumental change in every part of your life. It will eliminate trying to perform the Christian balancing act of budgeting time and effort for God, church, family, work, prayer, and the like. It will enable your words and your actions to become one. More importantly, you can be at peace with God as well as with your circumstances and the people in your life.

The bible says, "For thus saith the Lord of hosts; After the glory hath he sent me unto the nations which spoiled you: for he that toucheth you toucheth the apple of his eye." (Zechariah 2:8)

Unveiling Your Purpose

You will not succeed if you try to discover your purpose in your own way. The only way to have your purpose unveiled to you is through God. God made you and he knows every part of you. He is your creator and manufacturer. He alone can help you find out the divine reason for your existence.

The bible says, "You alone know when I sit down and when I get up. You read my thoughts from far away." (Psalm 139: 2 GW)

You will need to check in with the manufacturer so he can show you how you were supposed to function.

Everyone wants to know their purpose in life. They want to understand what they were put on earth to do. A life out of purpose is a penniless life. The day you understand purpose is the day of your greatest discovery. That's when you awaken out of slumber and start living.

Merely existing is not good. Merely existing is cheating your world out of your existence. Don't rob your generation of their blessings, which is you! Purpose means the original intent of a thing. When God created you He had something specific and special at the forefront of His mind.

There were problems in the world that he created you to solve. You can never experience fulfillment until you solve those problems. God never made anyone fail. He has success in mind for you. There are great victories for you to obtain and heights for you to attain.

The Bible says, "The hand of the diligent shall bear rule: but the slothful shall be under tribute." (Proverbs 12:24)

Whatever God has called you to do, do it with all your might. If He called you to preach and teach His Word, make sure you do that to the best of your ability before you get sidetracked on other responsibilities.

Make a move today. Accomplish something big for God. You can do it. You are unstoppable. The tide is turning in your favor. God has placed His bet on you and you are going to accomplish something great for God.

Chapter Three

Exploring Your Purpose

Not knowing your purpose opens the door to various forms of abuse including self-abuse. Take this time to ask yourself, "What is my Purpose?" Now ask God, "What is my purpose?" You need to know why God designed you to be here on this earth. Why did He strategically place you in your family whether it be a good reason or a bad reason, you deserve to know. I am sure at times, you wonder, "why do I go through the things that I go through?" "Why do others get away with things that I can never get away with?"

The book of Proverbs states, "Do you see a person who is efficient in his work? He will serve kings. He will not serve unknown people." (Proverbs 22:19 GW)

Remember, God is a God of purpose. He proposes, He plans, and then He manifests His plans in and throughout our lives. Our lives were set in motion in the book of Genesis with the words "In the beginning." Genesis 1:1. Our purpose began in the Garden of Eden when God said, "Let us make man in our own image." (Genesis 1:26).

This truly lets us know that there was a conversation in heaven about you regarding your life and everything you were going to do in and with your body. He knew every lie you were going to tell, every act of manipulation, fornication, and every bad habit you have encompassed throughout your life.

Basically, God knew every sin, transgression, and iniquity that we were going to commit with our bodies and this is why He sent His only begotten Son Jesus Christ to die on the cross. (Read Isaiah 53:5 and John 3:16)

Therefore, begin to search out your purpose and live the purpose filled life that God has already chosen for you.

You Must Make a difference

Life is not long enough to waste any minute of it. You must know your purpose so that you can maximize it. Knowing your purpose empowers you to live it out boldly and courageously. When we invest our lives and time wisely we can get a whole lot of results. Acting on information is much greater than the information itself.

Whatever God has called you to do, do it with all your might. If He called you to preach and teach His Word, make sure you do that to the best of your ability before you get sidetracked on other responsibilities.

Whatever you are doing, if you give up when you meet a little resistance, you will never achieve the level of success you are capable of achieving. This book is filled with good ideas that can really make a difference in your life, business, career or destiny -but only if you follow them with passion and purpose. The Bible says, "But be doers of the word and not hearers only, deceiving yourselves." (James 1:22)

Discovering Your Voice In Your Purpose

It's impossible to find purpose outside of God. Everything is centered on God who created the whole world and the millions of species living in them. God decided your life before you were born. The bible says, "You can make many plans, but the LORD's purpose will prevail." (Proverbs 19:21 NLT)

If you ask people, "Why do you exist?" most cannot tell you. They cannot explain their purpose in the world nor can they tell you the meaning of their life. This is a problem of catastrophic proportions.

It's a problem that I saw in the world and is the reason I wrote this book; so that many will read and find the meaning of their lives and discover God's purpose for their birth. Thank God for helping us walk in our purpose and anointing.

I encourage you to find your own unique voice in this noisy world. Everyday everyone is saying something. There's so much noise in the stratosphere. But God called your voice to be unique and different. Following your purpose and assignment is how you make your voice heard in the universe!

Finding your voice can be quite tricky, yet I encourage you to start recording your own voice! You can't be afraid or reluctant to listen to yourself. And even watch yourself as you speak, sing, dance, instruct or do whatever it is you do. When you watch yourself you can correct and make yourself better. Get comfortable with your own voice!

I'd like you to know that it's impossible to be on purpose and not prosper and be blessed. Please allow me to say this again, "The only reason people suffer and lack is because they are not in their divine purpose."

The meaning of your life is to live out your purpose on the earth. Your life is meaningless outside of your purpose. A lack of purpose is an epidemic in the world. God spoke concerning Moses, "But I have raised you up for this very purpose, that I might show you my power and that my name might be proclaimed in all the earth." (Exodus 9:16 NIV)

The meaning of your life is to serve God in His purpose for your life. That means you do everything that He wants you to do. Knowing

Jesus intimately becomes your greatest pursuit. What a glorious bliss to know Jesus intimately. He saved us so that we can serve Him and reach the world for Him. Unfortunately, we've all become so preoccupied with our own self-invented plans and ambitions that we fall short of the divine idea for our existence.

The meaning of your life is to succeed beyond your wildest dreams and imaginations. You came to be a bearer of hope to the world. God expects you to aspire to your highest aspirations.

Experience First Class Living

Knowing your purpose will help you to live a first class lifestyle without compromise. You deserve the first class of everything throughout your life. I know that might sound cheesy but it is so true. Royalty is inside of you.

God has planned for you to live a wonderful, blessed, electrifying and productive life. There is no iota of failure or suffering in God's divine idea for your life. Your existence on earth is a royal one full of divine privileges.

Apostle Peter writes, "But you are a chosen people, a royal priesthood, a holy nation, God's special possession, that you may declare the praises of him who called you out of darkness into his wonderful light." (1 Peter 2:9 NIV)

I encourage you today to take a stand to live a life of purpose and significance and to be all that you were created to be. I'm sure that by now you understand that you were created to be a solution to mankind's problems. Another thing that is interesting about you is that your birth was pre-planned and well thought out before you were even born. God wired you to live out divinity in your humanity. Purpose is all over you causing you to break forth on every side.

God has a special mission for you to do and you are going to need money to do it.

When your heartbeat is for the propagation of the gospel and the extension of God's kingdom, kingdom wealth will naturally follow you like bees follow honey. Even the scripture says that goodness and mercy shall follow you all the days of your life.

Chapter Four

God's Primary Purpose

Many times, we choose our own paths based on our surroundings, our communities, or what someone has told us. In this life we have been told that we were not good enough, tall enough, pretty enough, smart enough, etc. But all along, God has already set our lives in motion regardless of how others may feel about the exteriority of our being. God never intended for us to settle in abuse and live unfulfilled lives.

The bible says, "Bring everyone who is called by my name, whom I created for my glory, whom I formed and made." (Isaiah 43:7 GW)

There is a scripture in the bible that tells us that we are fearfully and wonderfully made Psalm 139:14. Let us take a moment to focus on the first part of that scripture, "I will praise you." We were created to seek God for our purpose and most importantly, praise Him in the process of our discovery. This simply means that our praise to God should never stop or be limited to our circumstances. Then, once we discover our purpose, our praise should be a continual praise of victory. I firmly believe that this is why so many people do not have a real praise towards God, because their praise is only based on a directive from a person telling them to "Praise God", and not what they were created to do or walk in from the beginning.

The last part of that scripture, "Your works are wonderful." This tells us that what God created, which is you and I, are wonderful and His only intent is to bless us immeasurably and to fill us with good things. However, when we don't know our purpose, we go through life settling for things that are not from God. We begin to feel like we cannot be happy for others when they are walking in their purpose.

Your Purpose is Precious To God

One of the main things about the divine idea for your purpose is that it is specific. God is not confused about what and who He created you to be and the problems you were born to solve. God's intention for your existence is precise to the dot. Allow me to take this a little deeper. It is not enough to understand that your purpose is to be a Doctor. What kind of a Doctor are you? Are you a surgeon? Are you a cardiologist? Or are you a neurologist?

Learning the specificity of your assignment will save you a lot of time and energy. This will prevent you from running the rat race and chasing every passion you can cook up.

We develop a mindset that limits the greatness of our God. We find ourselves stuck in time with no way of getting out. Nevertheless, I speak to you and tell you that from this day forward, you can and will come up and out of what has you limited and what is determined to control you. Our God is a God of breakthrough and because you are reading this book the Lord has broken forth purpose in your life at this very moment. Hallelujah!!!!

Don't go around trying to be all things to all people. You are not called to be everything to everyone. God has a specific purpose and assignment for your life.

Apostle Paul said, "I have not yet reached my goal, and I am not perfect. But Christ has taken hold of me. So I keep on running and struggling to take hold of the prize. My friends, I don't feel that I have already arrived. But I forget what is behind, and I struggle for what is ahead. I run toward the goal, so that I can win the prize of being called to heaven." (Philippians 3:12-14 CEV)

You Are A Designers Original

Because your purpose is unique and specific, it's necessary that you understand that you are not called to copy other people's success or failure. Your purpose is very different from some other people's purpose. God has called you to do something very specific and unique on the earth.

The bible says, "We wouldn't put ourselves in the same class with or compare ourselves to those who are bold enough to make their own recommendations. Certainly, when they measure themselves by themselves and compare themselves to themselves, they show how foolish they are. How can we brag about things that no one can evaluate? Instead, we will only brag about what God has given us to do—coming to the city of Corinth where you live." (2 Corinthians 10:12-13)

You must be true to the way God coded you. The way you were wired is different from everybody else. Stay true to yourself and have fun. Lower your shoulders a little bit, relax your face and let the sun shine on you.

You will only be judged by what God created you to do and not by what He created somebody else to do.

People's success or failure in life is not dependent on the color of your skin. Purpose is color blind. You can be white, black, green, brown or yellow. It doesn't matter. All that matters for your success is that you are in the center of God's will for your life. Don't be afraid of standing out. Be who you really are!

Pay attention to your life. Your purpose is screaming at you everywhere you turn. The problems you are assigned to solve are begging you to answer their cry. What pain moves you? What passion motivates you? Whose cry is distinct in your ears? What would you do if no one ever paid you for it?

What do you have incredible joy and excitement doing? What kinds of problems and opportunities always find their way to your space?

Many times, your purpose has shown up in your door step over and over again but you have neglected to see it for what it is.

Enjoying Your Purpose

When we're on purpose we naturally enjoy our lives and what we do. God wants you to enjoy every second of your life. Be intentional in enjoying your life and purpose. Jesus already suffered for you and me so that we can live for Him.

Apostle Paul said, "Charge them that are rich in this world, that they be not high minded, nor trust in uncertain riches, but in the living God, who giveth us richly all things to enjoy." (1 Timothy 6:17)

Success is birth out of purpose. Your purpose opens the doors of success and prosperity unto you. Life is easier when we are on purpose.

God will fund what He sponsors. When you are on purpose, you will enjoy God's provision and blessing. God's provision is a sign of His approval on what you are doing. You were made for God, not vice versa, and life is about letting God use you for His purposes, not using him for your own purpose.

Jesus said, "In the same way, let your good deeds shine out for all to see, so that everyone will praise your heavenly Father." (Matthew 5:16 NLT)

God will provide for you when you are on purpose. You will enjoy all the benefits of heaven. What seems hard for other people will be easy for you.

Purpose makes your life easy. God has destined you for greatness and all you have to do is to walk in it!

I encourage you today to walk in your blessed purpose and I promise that your life will dramatically change forever!

Chapter Five

Knowing Your Authenticity

Not knowing your purpose opens the door to confusion. Webster's dictionary declares confusion is a lack of understanding. It is factual that people have a lack of knowledge of who they really are. This is why so many human beings commit some of the most unfathomable things and then after the fact ask themselves, "What was I thinking?"

That remorseful feeling of wonder is our spirit man not agreeing with the situation or decision that we made in our flesh. Anytime anything makes you wonder how you could have handled a situation better, makes you cry, resent, or makes you feel a sense of resentment toward yourself, or another individual is not what God proposed for your life. In other words, it was not of God.

God will never do anything to hurt you. That is not His character. He gives us free will. Be mindful of what you do today that can affect your entire life. Many people never think about the consequences of the selfish acts they commit, and they can never fathom how it will affect their family, friends and loved ones until after the deed has been done.

Many people believe that if they grew up in a bad situation then that was the life that was chosen for them. This is not true at all concerning your life. How is it that most people born in opposition can overcome and achieve the best in life while others choose to sit and sulk in their situations? Decisions.

This lets us know that people choose to live the lives that they want to live. There's a scripture in the bible that says, "And we know that all things work together for good to them that love God, to them who are called according to His purpose." (Romans 8:28)

Here are some tips that would help you in your great discovery:

It All Begins with God

God knows who you really are because He created you. Knowing who you are begins with God. Society will lie to you just to make you fold into their mold.

The search for purpose and personal discovery has puzzled people for thousands of years.

Many have resulted to invent their own sense of purpose. Purpose begins with God. You didn't form yourself so you are not authorized to create a path for your life without consulting with your Maker. Let God show you the path He has already carved out for you. Like a master wood-carver, He has the chisel in His hand and wisely creates the impressions in His mind within wood for the world to see and emulate.

The bible says, "I will praise You, for I am fearfully and wonderfully made; Marvelous are Your works, and that my soul knows very well." Psalms 139:14

He is the perfection of beauty. If you want to have a life of significance, ask God to reveal to you His purpose for your life. It's really that simple.

The bible says, "If any of you is deficient in wisdom, let him ask of the giving God [Who gives] to everyone liberally and ungrudgingly, without reproach or faultfinding and it will be given him." (James 1:5 AMP)

God has not left us guessing about our reason for existence. He has not left us in the dark. His Spirit is there to lead us and His Word is there to guide us.

Always Go to the Manufacturer

God is your manufacturer. He wired and brought you into existence. He alone holds the key to your great destiny. God works in the good and bad on our behalf, but we must choose the path that we are willing to take.

You will either choose His way or the way of your surroundings. Your environment does not have to dictate who you can become. You were destined for greatness! It's only the manufacturer of a product that knows how a product is supposed to function. The manual contains the pre-programmed functions of the product. For us as Christians our manual is the bible and our manufacturer is God. God is flawless and He is the epitome of perfection. Everything He does is beautiful and flawless just like Him.

Stay Razor Sharp Focused on Purpose

One of the strategies of the enemy against my life has been to try to take me out of purpose. I have fought and resisted the urge to lose focus of who I really am in Christ. It is amazing how much life can be simpler when we all stay focused on our purpose and assignment. Staying focused helps you not to see what your adversaries are saying about you or doing to you. If your eyes are single, your whole body will be full of light.

Don't focus on your past. Your past is your past and there is nothing you can do about it. But you can focus on the glorious future that God has for you. Your future is way better than your past. What God has for you is prettier than what the devil did to you a few years back.

Apostle Paul told us to run our race as skilled athletes. Skilled athletes have no time to wonder about what people around them are plotting. They keep their mind and eyes on the finish line. Stay put and engrossed in your purpose and know who you are. God is working it out for your good and your advantage.

The bible says, "For it is God which worketh in you both to will and to do of his good pleasure." Philippians 2:13

Cast Down Fear

Do you know the main reason God created you? It wasn't so you could pursue your personal dreams or goals, career or hobby aside from His purpose for your life. You were made to worship Jesus Christ; the Son of God and Son of Man. You were made to praise His name and accomplish His purpose on earth.

Fear will try to make you doubt who you are. When God says you can do it, fear will question your belief in God!

Sadly, many lives are driven by pain, guilt, fear, insecurity, approval, addiction, paychecks, bills, fame, competition or even condemnation. Our lives are supposed to be purpose driven. The Bible says, "For God has not given us a spirit of fear, but of power and of love and of a sound mind." (2 Timothy 1:7)

The bible says, "Then the Lord answered me and said: "Write the vision and make it plain on tablets, That he may run who reads it." (Habakkuk 2:2)

The Bible says, "We walk by faith and not by sight." (2 Corinthians 5:7)

Fear is a robber of destinies. Fear has destroyed great dreams and dreamers. I have seen fear reduce the giants of men to midgets. General Colin Powell, in my opinion, could have been the first black president of America but the fear of being assassinated prevented him from pursuing the high office.

The ten spies missed out of Canaan and lost the battle of courage because they welcomed fear into their hearts. Joshua and Caleb ignored their fear and experienced the blessings of God. The Bible exposes fear as a tormentor. The bible says, "There is no fear in love; but perfect love casts out fear, because fear involves torment. But he who fears has not been made perfect in love." (1 John 4:18)

Every disadvantage also has an advantage connected with it. You are the one that God has chosen for the task and God never made a mistake with your purpose. Go and shine! Beat fear and don't allow it to hold you prisoner!

Chapter Six

Look Beyond Your Situation

Not knowing your purpose blinds your vision. I must say that if you're reading this book, you are not blind. However, how many times have we sensed or seen the negative signs about a person or a situation, but went along with it thinking we can change the person or the situation? In the end we always wish that we had not gotten ourselves involved in the situation in the first place.

This usually happens when you don't know your purpose. When our purpose is of God, it comes with no sorrow. (Proverbs 10:22) Not only is this scripture talking about money, it is also referring to a wealth of peace, a wealth of joy, a wealth of happiness, a wealth of love, a wealth of good health and a wealth of fulfillment.

I encourage you to pause right now and give God praise in advance because as you continue reading this book you are stepping into your God given purpose. Hallelujah!!!

You must know your purpose in every situation that you are placed in. You must know this without a doubt. Ask yourself, "Am I happy in what I am involved in and is this bringing me fulfillment?" If not, then this could mean you have a lack of knowledge of your purpose. Doing things our own way does not position us for the purpose that God has for our lives.

I am going to share another real-life story with you. I was told that from a baby I was ready for the world. Always a go-getter. A leader always younger than my peers. I was going to make things happen no matter what it took. I was going to make people and their lives better.

The bible says, "There is a way which seemeth right unto a man, but the end thereof are the ways of death." Proverbs 14:12

However, when I became a young adult and dating, I thought I could change a man despite me being warned by others and seeing the signs myself. I tell you the truth, it only left me hurt, unappreciated, bewildered and totally disappointed.

All that I had put into the relationship, including doing wifely duties for a boyfriend, was not God's purpose for my life. Just for the mere fact that I was doing this in my own right was a recipe for disaster. Discouragements have an interesting way of narrowing your focus and bringing clarity to your purpose. People might have given up on you because of some past situations but don't give up on yourself. God is not through with you. Greater is he that is in you than he that is in the world. Believe and receive!

Maximize Your Vision

When you consistently visualize your purpose coming to pass, you release God's creative powers to work for you to bring it to pass. Abraham visualized his future. He saw his purpose before anyone else did.

Sometimes you will have to see your purpose alone before other people see it with you.

Abraham saw beyond his past situation of childlessness. He believed God even when other people were laughing and mocking him. God can take you further than you ever imagined.

The Bible says, "After Lot separated from him, God said to Abram, "Open your eyes, look around. Look north, south, east, and west. Everything you see, the whole land spread out before you, I will give to you and your children forever. I'll make your descendants like dust—counting your descendants will be as impossible as counting the dust of the Earth. So—on your feet, get moving! Walk through the country, its length and breadth; I'm giving it all to you. Abram moved his tent. He went and settled by the Oaks of Mamre in Hebron. There he built an altar to God." Genesis 13:14-18 (MSG)

The power of vision can't be overstated. It's the antidote to attaining life's maximum. Enlarge your vision and step into it with boldness and confidence.

See yourself beyond the pain and abuse of your childhood. Know that God is going to use everything you have been through to promote you.

See your new house, car, job, career and lifestyle with the eyes of your spirit. See what God is about to do for you!

The devil likes to confuse us. He likes to see us defeated and live without purpose and direction. This is one of the reasons I wrote this book so that you can see what your purpose in God is and start walking in it. Like I said earlier, a life without purpose is a wasted life. A life without a sense of purpose is one that is open to abuse and all kinds of demonic intrusions. I pray that God will begin to open your eyes so that you really know and appreciate who you are in God and accomplish all that heaven has destined for you. I believe this is your time and season. God is just getting started with you.

You Are Chosen and Ordained

Your purpose in life is chosen and ordained by God. It is not negotiable. God had a plan in mind when He allowed your spirit, which was in heaven, to come into flesh and blood and be born on earth. "The Lord will fulfill his purpose for me" (Psalms 138:8).

God's purpose for your life never changes, but you have to make up your mind to fulfill it.

Psalms tells us that "I have an assigned portion (purpose and destiny). LORD, you have assigned me my portion and my cup; you have made my lot secure. The boundary lines have fallen for me in pleasant places; surely I have a delightful inheritance" (Psalms 16:5-6).

At one time in our lives, we all had a vision for the quality of life that we desire and deserve. Yet, for many of us, those dreams have become so shrouded in the frustrations and routines of daily life that we no longer make an effort to accomplish them.

For far too many, the dream has dissipated, and with it so has the will to shape our destinies. How many have lost that sense of certainty that creates the winner's edge. My burning desire is to restore your yearning for purpose.

The Power of Self Affirmation

Self-affirmation is a habit of successful people. There's a segment of your brain that registers your voice dictations better and faster than the voice of someone else. Remember I told you that there are people that have heard so many negative words growing up, they've paid attention to too many negative thoughts, they've had too many negative experiences and those things have shaped them and formed them to the point that they doubt that greatness can be achieved.

The only way to truly win this battle is to implement the habit of self-affirmation.

The bible says, "I can do all things through Christ which strengtheneth me." (Philippians 4:13)

That self-affirmation must be rooted in God's Spirit filled words because His words are the only things that cut apart negative experiences and words permanently. If you never tell your brain who you are, society and its norms will define you. So every morning I declare God's word over my life in order to shape my life.

The Bible says, "Death and life are in the power of the tongue, And those who love it will eat its fruit." (Proverbs 18:21)

Your purpose in life is not something that you invent; it is something that you discover. Your purpose brings discipline and focus into your life.

Chapter Seven

What Is Your Role?

We have to know our purpose and fulfill it to the maximum of our capabilities. When you know your purpose, you will then become positioned for greatness.

Let us break down a very familiar passage of scripture John 8:1-11 about a woman in the bible that was caught in adultery. Whatever her circumstances were during that time that drove her to that lifestyle of being an adulterer ultimately positioned her before Jesus. The bible says that the teachers of the law and the Pharisee's threw her down on the ground before Jesus' feet after being caught in the very act of adultery.

The bible also says that they questioned Jesus as to what the law stated. The law stated that she was to be stoned to death. Jesus, knowing his God given purpose stooped down and began writing in the sand with his finger. While writing, Jesus clearly verbalized a statement saying, "He who is without sin cast the first stone at her."

Being that no human being on earth then, and now, is without sin, we know that no one could honestly cast the first stone. Moreover, what the teachers of the law and the Pharisees did not realize is that they positioned her for purpose.

In my opinion, she preached one of the greatest sermons after Jesus' resurrection exclaiming, "He Lives!" "He Lives!"

The bible says, "And as they went to tell his disciples, behold, Jesus met them, saying, All hail. And they came and held him by the feet, and worshiped him." (Matthew 28:9)

So, you see, regardless of what you are going through or regardless of your past, you can still go to God and ask Him to show you your purpose. And He will be more than glad to show you.

What are some things that you have gone through in your life that can make you truly say, "God positioned me for purpose?"

Knowing your purpose will give you peace in the midst of any storm and after the storm settles, you will still be standing. The storms of life come to weigh us down and throw us off course, but knowing your purpose brings an indescribable peace from within that will help you to withstand any storm knowing that the God almighty is on your side.

The bible says, "Then they cry unto the Lord in their trouble, and he bringeth them out of their distresses. He maketh the storm calm, so that the waves thereof are still. Then are they glad because they are quiet; so he bringeth them unto their desired haven." Psalm 107:29

Positioned for Greatness

Your purpose determines your position in life. Without purpose, relationships cannot be maximized.

Your purpose requires other people to help you to realize it. The same way other people need you in order for them to fulfill their purpose as well. You were not designed by God to fulfill it on your own.

Purpose helpers are those relationships that God aligns with our lives and destinies to help us to succeed in our purpose.

Believe me when I tell you that there are people that are assigned to your purpose. They are purposeful helpers. When God was coding your purpose He considered the people He will use to attain it. Everything and everyone you need were already created by God.

God's purpose for your life is so far greater than what you could do by yourself. You'll need the participation, involvement and resources of other people to undertake it.

The scripture says, "As iron sharpens iron, so one person sharpens another." (Proverbs 27:17 NIV)

Your purpose helpers understand your calling. These are the kinds of people that love you unconditionally.

Jesus had the twelve disciples to help him fulfill his assignment on the earth. Paul had Timothy and Barnabas. David has Samuel. Do you know the people that God had positioned in your life to help your purpose journey?

Stay in Position

Looking back at my life I can see how trials and circumstances came against me to make me lose my position in my purpose. Even till this day I have to remind myself to stay on purpose.

Jesus said it best in, "The thief cometh not, but for to steal, and to kill, and to destroy: I am come that they might have life, and that they might have it more abundantly." (John 10:10)

Keep on moving in spite of whatever pain, hurts, setbacks or discouragements that come to you. The strongest people aren't the people who win, but the people who don't give up when others think they lost. The race of life is not for the best but for the brave. They are the ones who know that God has called them to success, and nothing can stop that divine will.

Sometimes, God will place you in situations in which you have no natural gifting. In these cases, God puts you there to experience His power in order to accomplish your tasks. This is a season of character building.

The bible says, "They shall run like mighty men; they shall climb the wall like men of war; and they shall march everyone on his ways, and they shall not break their ranks: Neither shall one thrust another; they shall walk everyone in his path: and when they fall upon the

sword, they shall not be wounded. They shall run to and fro in the city; they shall run upon the wall; they shall climb up upon the houses; they shall enter in at the windows like a thief." (Joel 2:7-9)

Look at Joseph in the bible, he went through a thirteen-year season of character building and preparation for purpose. It was hardly an "assignment" that matched his purpose it might seem. But the process to fulfill his primary assignment included this painful process. This is how a young boy without a formal education could become a successful prime minister of Egypt.

Like I said earlier, most of the successful people we all recognize today didn't start out to be great or successful. They simply followed their passion and purpose. They either experienced problems in their personal lives or in the society that pulled out their purpose. In each case they were thrust into a circumstance not of their choosing that led to their ultimate assignment in life that was rooted in their purpose. You cannot force that timetable. It is up to God when that time is just right.

Do Not Be A People Pleaser

Your positioning in God will offend some people. No matter how much you try to carry everyone along it's impossible to make everyone happy about your purpose. I made the mistake of trying so hard to please everyone and make everyone happy, but I failed woefully in the task. It is not your job or mine to make people happy. You just do what God called you to do and let God take care of the rest.

Let me say up front that people pleasers do not attain their purpose. Your purpose will offend some people. They will not like it or believe in it. To be significant and successful in your purpose you will have to be comfortable with people not liking you. Purposeful people don't care much about what other people think about them.

Chapter Eight

Shift The Trajectory of Your Mindset

Knowing your purpose will allow you to embrace adversity. When you can embrace adversity, you can conquer anything with the help of Jesus Christ. Jesus was determined and purposed to carry us to the cross. Therefore, with Him and through Him we can conquer anything. (John 19:1-42)

There is a scripture that declares, "With man things are impossible, but with God all things are possible." (Matthew 19:26)

That means that it is possible to walk in your purpose with God on your side. Knowing your purpose changes everything. You begin to think bigger and your passion for God's purpose grows stronger on the inside of you each day.

You begin to talk to Him every day asking Him of His next assignment for your life. You begin to change your surroundings for the better. You will also gain freedom knowing that you are no longer controlled by others nor your circumstances. Not even your emotions have dominion over you any longer. Your life will never be the same. Hallelujah!!!

I am inclined to tell you that the best thing that could have ever happened in my life was when I discovered my purpose. It took me many years, but I overcame it and found out who I really was. What I initially thought was my purpose kept me bound in the mindset of always trying to make someone else's life better.

I was unknowingly neglecting myself, my purpose, my spiritual growth and wearing myself out physically. Our only job on this earth is to seek the Master for our purpose, praise Him for His revelation, and run in it like we have never ran before. You may feel like you are too old or that you are too far behind in the race to complete your purpose. But dismiss that thought today!

The bible declares, "That the race is not given to the swift or to the strong, but to those who endure to the end." (Ecclesiastes 9:11)

You have the endurance! Gold gets better and more precious when it passes through the fire. The fire purifies it and gets the impurities out. The devil usually sends us discouragements to hinder us but God uses it to build our strength and character.

Change Is Imperative

The easiest thing to do is to run during times of testing and trials. But I'd like you to know that you can never conquer what you are not willing to confront. Running away from your purpose is futile. God will always have a way to bring you into your position and purpose. We tend to run because we don't want to undergo the pain of change.

Pain is necessary for change. Pain is also necessary for growth. Where there is no change it means that person is not growing.

The bible says, "I beseech you therefore, brethren, by the mercies of God, that ye present your bodies a living sacrifice, holy, acceptable unto God, which is your reasonable service. And be not conformed to this world: but be ye transformed by the renewing of your mind, that ye may prove what is that good, and acceptable, and perfect, will of God." (Romans 12:1-2)

Do you really believe what you say you believe? Do you believe what you think you believe? Don't be so quick to answer the questions until you have tasted the teas of adversities and discouragements. The strength of a tea is when it is in hot water.

That is when what is on the inside shows. God will allow discouragement to come in to test your convictions in your purpose. Don't quit in times of trial and change. It's only a test!

God Heals Disappointments

There is nothing that draws us closer to Godlike discouragements do. Embracing the changes that God wants you to make might bring some disappointments along the way. It is important that you know how to handle the pain of disappointments.

All disappointments are a blessing because when we're discouraged, we have no one to turn to but God.

King David said, "From the end of the earth will I cry unto thee, when my heart is overwhelmed: lead me to the rock that is higher than I." (Psalms 61:2)

Disappointments and setbacks don't mean that you are losing; in fact the opposite is true.

Disappointments bring clarity and renewed focus to us. When I look back at my life over the years, I have seen the places where I felt disappointments and discouragements but now that I am properly positioned in my purpose I can honestly thank God for those tough seasons because they helped to shape and mold me into the woman of God that I am today.

Paul said, "Yea doubtless, and I count all things but loss for the excellency of the knowledge of Christ Jesus my Lord: for whom I have suf ered the loss of all things, and do count them but dung, that I may win Christ,And be found in him, not having mine own righteousness, which is of the law, but that which is through the faith of Christ, the righteousness which is of God by faith:" (Philippians 3:8-9)

Discouragements have an interesting way of narrowing our focus and bringing clarity to your purpose.

Beauty for Ashes

God is a master at bringing our strengths out of weaknesses. When you call yourself small it is because you haven't seen the greatness that is possible with you. One thing about people I don't like is that oftentimes, people are so quick to judge and define us. I am here to tell you today that in every disability in your life lie your true abilities.

The bible says, "To appoint unto them that mourn in Zion, to give unto them beauty for ashes, the oil of joy for mourning, the garment of praise for the spirit of heaviness; that they might be called trees of righteousness, the planting of the Lord, that he might be glorified." (Isaiah 61:3)

For instance, if you're experiencing financial issues right now, it could be that you have a gift for prosperity and God is still training you in prosperity. After all, no military wants to place an untested and untrained soldier on the battlefield. Some of the greatest people that the world has ever known had profound disabilities. And in those disabilities they found their true calling and purpose.

Jesus was born in a mere manger without any natural financial or social connections and yet in that limited earthly resource He learnt how to trade His earthly disabilities for the divine abilities of God.

All you have to do when you find any situation in your life, whether it is financial, emotional, economical, mental, societal or relational is to trade your weakness for God's strength. Do not allow your life to be limited to your weaknesses.

Chapter Nine

Moving Loud In Your Purpose

Jesus is eagerly waiting for you to walk in your purpose so that He can lead and guide you every step.

The bible says, "The thief comes not but to kill, steal and to destroy. But, Jesus declares that I have come that you might have life and have it more abundantly. " (John 10:10)

This tells us that Satan is the thief that has stolen from us for far too long. Satan has stolen our children, our marriages, our possessions and any other thing that has any level of significance to us. However, most of this occurred because we did not or do not know our purpose in God.

The bible lets us know throughout history that God had already preordained and purposed our lives over two thousand years ago. I pray that as you continue to read this book, God will begin to unlock every possibility regarding your purpose. I pray that every gift and talent you possess will operate under the anointing of the Most High. I pray that you will not only operate in your gifts and talents, but that you will function under the authority of the heart of Jesus while operating in your purpose.

I would like to remind you that as you begin to walk in your purpose you will encounter some problems and resistance along the way. Purpose and problems go together. Problems are an opportunity for purpose. If there was not the problem of Saul disobeying God,

David would not have come into his full purpose to be king. Even giants in our lives help us to shine through into our purpose. They help us to focus and dig deeper to pull out what was hidden within us all along.

A Christian that is driven by purpose makes a difference at church and everywhere they go. We are called to be difference makers.

Apostle John rightly states, "That which was from the beginning, which we have heard, which we have seen with our eyes, which we have looked upon, and our hands have handled, concerning the Word of life—the life was manifested, and we have seen, and bear witness, and declare to you that eternal life which was with the Father and was manifested to us— that which we have seen and heard we declare to you, that you also may have fellowship with us; and truly our fellowship is with the Father and with His Son Jesus Christ. And these things we write to you that your joy may be full." (1 John 1:1-4)

Your Purpose Will speak For You

Walking in your purpose involves prophesying your purpose. You've got to speak it out of your mouth on a daily basis. When you prophesy your purpose, you are agreeing with God and activating and mobilizing angels and heavenly hosts to work behind the scenes to actualize your purpose.

Look at David who had already defeated Goliath through his words even before the battle began. David understood that words have power and our mouths can release prophecies into our future.

David said to Saul, "Your servant has killed both lion and bear; and this uncircumcised Philistine will be like one of them, seeing he has defied the armies of the living God." (1 Samuel 17:36)

A prophecy means that you are calling those things that are not as though they are. You are looking at an empty bank account and prophesying it full.

We need to understand that our words carry prophetic power. It carries an inherent power that cannot be subdued. When you say constructive things, those things begin to happen to you. Likewise when you open your mouth and you say negative things, those negative things happen to you. It's not by chance nor is it by coincidence; it's because of what you have opened your mouth to say. Where do you see yourself five years from now? Start talking about it now.

Declare Those Things

You are an asset to the Kingdom and God has a need for you. Declare out of your own mouth this day, "I am walking in my purpose."

The bible says that, "we can say things are not as though they were." (Romans 4:17)

Begin to declare life into your purpose every day and watch the turnaround of rewards manifest.

Speak life to your family, your business, your body, your finances, your ministry, and whatever is lying dormant that you know should be up and functioning and bringing you happiness and fulfillment.

Every enviable dreamer has a big mouth. The enemy is not really after you. He is after your big mouth. The devil wants to silence you and prevent you from talking. The power of your dreams is in your mouth.

You have creative ability in you. You are an expression of God's divinity.

An extraordinary being! Lift your head high. There are seeds of greatness inside of you. Speak it!

Leap Out in Faith

God is waiting for you to start walking in your purpose. Life is too short to sit down and do nothing with your purpose. There's not enough time to sit around and do nothing spectacular with your life. You're on a mission with God. You're on a mission to live out your purpose and change the world.

The scripture says, "The created world itself can hardly wait for what's coming next." (Romans 8:19 MSG)

Use every gift, talent, idea and skill that God gave you for the glory of His name and change your world.

The world is waiting for you to rise up and solve the problems that you were born to do.

God's purpose for our lives is always larger than our biggest dreams and aspirations. His divine idea for our existence is so gigantic that it often leaves us wondering in our thoughts if we could ever attain and satisfy it.

The bible says, "For we walk by faith, not by sight:" (2 Corinthians 5:7)

But I want to tell you that it is doable. God will never give you more than you can handle. He will never leave or forsake us. You cannot live out a purpose that you don't believe in. step out in faith and make your life awesome.

Have faith in God's ability to accomplish great things through you. Stop undermining yourself as being insignificant. God never made anything that was insignificant. You were born with purpose and destiny.

Your life is greater than you see right now. Believe in your purpose, believe in your dreams and believe in yourself. Receive the grace and anointing to function in your purpose.

Think like God thinks about you.

The bible says, "For as he thinks in his heart, so is he..." (Proverbs 23:7)

Chapter Ten

The Journey of Your Purpose

God's desire is for you to know your purpose and to walk in your purpose. He desires to get the glory out

of your life. No longer are you going to allow the enemy to sidetrack you and destroy your purpose. You will not be one of those the enemy can distract from your purpose any longer.

I prophesy greater purpose over your life from this day forward in Jesus Name. In all that has been discussed in this book make sure that your purpose is connected to God. Make a conscious decision to keep your purpose clear with pure intentions toward God.

Please know that God is your source, your creator, and your way maker. His purpose will always breed success. When your purpose lines up with His Word, His Word has no choice but to back you up because He is a man that shall not lie; (Numbers 23:19).

Prepare yourself for the abundant overflow of God's blessings. The Old Testament declares what God has purposed and planned for our lives.

Please read Deuteronomy 8:1-20. This will remind you of God's promises when we obey and walk in our God given purpose.

Let this day be a reminder to you that whatever situation you find yourself in, know that your God given purpose will ignite peace and fulfillment.

You were made for an awesome life. You were born to reflect the glory of the lord. When I understood clearly that God's provision for my life, ministry, and destiny is tied to my purpose I was excited. I got it that God will never sponsor a project that He wouldn't pay for.

My existence was never my idea, it was God's idea. He brought you and I into this world for His vision for the earth. Wouldn't you think He will provide for His own plan? Of course he would!

Everyone wants to know their purpose in life. They want to understand what they were put on earth to do. It is good to know that God finishes a product in the spirit before He begins to manufacture it. I have to remind you again that your purpose was completed before you started it.

God is proud of you. The day you understand purpose is the day of your great discovery. That's when you awaken out of slumber and start living. Merely existing is cheating your world out of your existence. Make the world feel your presence and entrance into the world. A life out of purpose is a pointless life.

Jesus says, "And he said unto them, Go ye into all the world, and preach the gospel to every creature. He that believeth and is baptized shall be saved; but he that believeth not shall be damned. And these signs shall follow them that believe; In my name shall they cast out devils; they shall speak with new tongues; They shall take up serpents; and if they drink any deadly thing, it shall not hurt them; they shall lay hands on the sick, and they shall recover. So then after the Lord had spoken unto them, he was received up into heaven, and sat on the right hand of God. And they went forth, and preached everywhere, the Lord working with them, and confirming the word with signs following. Amen." (Mark 16:15-20)

Purpose Commingled With Provision

The provisions of God are in your place of purpose. Your place of purpose is your assignment, including the geographical location of your assignment. The concept of purpose and provisions is so very powerful.

The bible says, "According as his divine power hath given unto us all things that pertain unto life and godliness, through the knowledge of him that hath called us to glory and virtue:" (2 Peter 1:3)

God has better things to do than to create you to fail or live out a mediocre, unexciting and fruitless life. God doesn't waste His time and so He didn't waste His time forming you and coding your purpose. Wake up from the fears and hindrances that have hindered your sense of purpose and identity.

No matter how small your purpose appears to be, within it is enough provisions to last your entire lifetime. There is provision for you and it is hidden in your purpose.

In this season pay attention to the voice of the Holy Spirit. God will speak to you and direct you to your purpose and provisions. You will need to be extra sensitive to the voice of God so that you don't miss your purpose, identity or positioning in this life.

Jesus said, "And when he brings out his own sheep, he goes before them; and the sheep follow him, for they know his voice." (John 10:4)

Whenever God speaks to you, act on it. He knows more about your purpose than you understand about it. He created your purpose, and He knows how to lead you in it. All you have to do is to follow His leadings, voice and instructions, especially when it doesn't make any sense. Build an intimate relationship with the Holy Spirit. This means, spending time with Him every day, singing and making melodies in your heart to the Lord. The more you spend time with someone the more distinct their voice will be to you.

In my closing I will leave you with principles that will help you understand your purpose in God.

Principles and Reflection

You've made it to the end of the book. I believe God that your life is changing, and you are on your way to a great discovery.

As you are discovering, all you have to do is to release and unleash your purpose to the world. Your purpose is so fundamental to who you are. This divine idea for your existence is so exciting and enriching to all that come in contact with you.

Your purpose may look small in your eyes, but it is mighty in the eyes of God. Don't underestimate the reason you were born. You can accomplish great things in your life.

Dream a big dream and go out and do it. God is setting you up for a mighty breakthrough. The test of perseverance is the one that many people cannot endure. All too often, they will move when God tells them to be still and wait. They will decide that they have been waiting long enough, so they set out to deliver themselves. This is a big mistake. If God has not completed the deeper work in you, He will take you around the mountain one more time-or even more if that is what is necessary to complete the inner work that He has begun in your life.

The bible says, "For in him we live and move and have our being.' As some of your own poets have said, 'We are his of spring.'" (Acts 17:28 NIV)

I allowed abuses in my life in the past because I was not following my purpose and calling, but thank God for opening my spiritual eyes so that I can behold and embrace my beautiful purpose.

I allowed the enemy to lie to me about my identity. I thought my purpose was intertwined with my boyfriends, career, and other things but now I realize that my real identity is in Christ and He alone can release me into my greatest potential.

What are some things you learned about yourself that you are now willing to make changes in your life for the better?

Principles

1. Not knowing my purpose can breed multiple identity crises.

   I Corinthians 14:33

2. Confusion of my purpose can destroy my destiny.

   Isaiah 41:10

3. My God given purpose births vision.

   Habakkuk 2:2, Proverbs 29:18

4. Understanding my purpose positions me for greatness.
   Jude 1:20-21
5. "When Purpose Is Not Known, Abuse Is Inescapable and Unavoidable"

What is Your Purpose For Kingdom?

_____

_____

_____

_____

_____

_____

_____

Identify your strengths and weaknesses to help you identify your purpose

_____

_____

_____

_____

_____

_____

_____

_____

_____

_____

_____

_____

_____

_____

_____

_____

_____

What are some mindset changes you need to make so that your purpose can be fulfilled?

_____

_____

_____

_____

_____

_____

_____

_____

_____

_____

_____

_____

_____

_____

_____

_____

_____

What are some goals you can set to help in your petitioning to God for your Purpose?

_____

_____

_____

_____

_____

_____

_____

_____

_____

_____

_____

_____

_____

_____

_____

_____

_____

List some mentors that you can learn from that are similar to you and your purpose.

_____

_____

_____

_____

_____

_____

_____

_____

_____

_____

_____

_____

_____

_____

_____

_____

_____

_____

_____

About Dr. Crystal S. Pugh

Dr. Crystal S. Pugh is a prominent author, dynamic speaker, educator, song writer, and entrepreneur. The beauty in which God has given her is coupled with grace, elegance, and poise when she mounts diverse platforms.

Dr. Crystal is a woman of God with a passion to see God's people discover the qualities of their purpose to which God has preordained for their lives.

She empowers and ignites the people of God to make life changing decisions through her teachings with the leading of the Holy Spirit.

Dr. Crystal has a prolific women's ministry focuses specifically on the original woman, instructing them to push from the pain of their past.

For More Information & Bookings EMAIL:

crystalpughministries@gmail.com

"Not knowing your purpose can breed multiple identity crises"